I0471610

Plant a Money Tree

Understanding Investment Options That Will
Give You Financial Independence

By K.C. Smith

Table of Contents

Introduction

It does not take years of hard labor to become a multimillionaire! If you don't believe me ask people like Warren Buffet who has spent the majority of his career in investment and became a millionaire at the age of 30! He has mastered the art of investing and could retire today if he wished and live off the interest.

There are two major reasons why people don't invest their money; first, they don't understand investing, and second, they are too scared to take the risk. What if I told you that even if you are on minimum wage, you can invest as little as 10% of your monthly earnings and become extremely wealthy!

This is not a get rich quick guide; it is not a lottery ticket so if that is what you are looking for you might as well close the book now. If you want to be successful in any area of your life it takes diligence and hard work, this book will teach you how to invest effectively so that you can make your money work for you and secure your future.

Over the last 100 years, the annual return of the S&P 500, which includes dividends, has been a little over 10%. Making the assumption that a onetime investment of $30,000 would grow to more than $1,000,000 within 37 years. The majority of people are unable to make that type of investment; however, making small monthly investments combined with the power of compound interest can increase your wealth substantially. An investment of $450 a month will turn into 2.5 million within a few decades.

Compound interest ensures that you receive a phenomenal return on your investment. If $30,000 turns into $1 million within 37 years without compound interest, the same amount of money left to grow over 45 years with compound interest at the same annual 10% rate will grow to more than double the figure at $2,186,00!

One of the greatest fears for new investors is that the stock market will crash. However, what people fail to realize is that regardless of a crash, you will still average approximately 10% over time. The most renowned investors such as Warren Buffet don't waste time trying to predict when the next crash is going to take place, that would be a waste of time as it is impossible to do.

Regardless of whether there is a crash in the market or not he knows that even the worst crash will be a small bump in the road because he is investing for the long haul. This is due to the power of compound interest, according to Albert Einstein; it is the most powerful force on the planet!

There is no high risk associated with compound interest; all it requires is that your funds are placed in an S&P Index Fund and left to grow. It isn't necessary to invest in the stock market to create wealth, there are several investment tools that when applied will make you a millionaire by the time you retire.

Investing and speculating are two completely different concepts. Playing the risky stock market game of buying low and selling high is really no different than gambling. People get addicted to the thrill of trying to beat the market and that is how they end up losing their hard earned cash. Forex trading is a plague to the investment industry and I would advise you not to get caught up in a system that offers odds that are worse than your local casino! True investing is not about making quick money; rather it focuses on long term intelligent decisions with consistent growth over a certain time period.

With the advances in technology, people have been able to effectively educate themselves on various investment opportunities. Achieving financial independence is the main goal for the majority of people and most people must work for the basic necessities of life and to enjoy luxuries such as cars, gadgets and vacations.

Saving for the future becomes extremely difficult when every penny is accounted for at the end of the month. Without being able to save money there will be none when it is needed the most for things such as your children's education, retirement, and unexpected emergencies.

Regardless of how modest your income, there are still ways that you can make your money work for you without drastically changing your life circumstances. Earning a second income through smart investing is a viable option for anyone regardless of their current financial situation.

For families or individuals with a modest income becoming wealthy seems like a dream that will never come to reality. However, investing your money is one of the best decisions you will ever make if you are patient enough to wait for a return on your investment.

Once again, investing is not a get rich quick gimmick this book is not going to teach you how to become a millionaire in 7 days. I like to say that investing takes investment, and that investment is the time that you spend educating yourself on the most effective methods of creating your own personal money tree.

Chapter 1: The Basics of Investment

The modern world is replete with a variety of complicated investment options; this makes it easy to lose the true essence of what it means to invest. Here is a simple parable to help you understand investment.

Bob and Mike are both farmers who live next door to each other. Bob has been very successful in his farming business and has saved enough food that he and his family will have enough to eat for the next 10 years. Being a sensible farmer, he would still like to exchange food today so that he will have food in the future just in case something happened and he was no longer able to work.

Mike has just started in the farming industry; he would like to have the security that Bob has. His desire is to spend enough time working on the farm so that he can build a new barn and expand his business so that he can save for the future. The dilemma that Mike faces is that if he spends time on the farm, he will not be able to harvest his crops for the year which means that his family will have no food to eat.

What Mike needs is to get his hands on extra food now so that he can produce more food in the future. Since Mike and Bob are neighbors, it only makes sense to borrow from Bob. However, before Bob parts with his food, he wants to make sure that he will get back more in the future than what he is giving up now. Bob also has the right to be concerned that Mike will take his food and disappear meaning that he loses out on his investment. Bob starts thinking about the proposition, but his thoughts are now centered on whether he could get a better deal from another farmer.

We are now going to look at stocks and bonds, and they represent two different ways that Bob and Mike could come to an agreement that will benefit both of them.

Bob could give Mike 200 bundles of wheat for 10% ownership in the new farm. If the investment made in the farm was successful, Bob would get much more back than the 200 bundles of wheat originally invested. If things don't turn out according to plan for Mike, Bob would risk losing his initial investment. In the finance world, this type of investing is referred to as a stock.

Stocks

If a survey was to be conducted and the layman was asked to explain investment, the majority of people would say it involves trading on the stock market. The stock market is one of many investment avenues. It is an economic concept which involves businesses selling parts of their assets in the form of stocks. An investor buys the stock which means that they are essentially giving the company a loan. The organization uses that money to invest in the growth of their business to make more money which increases the value of their stocks. When the value of the stocks increase, investors make a profit by selling their stocks at a higher price.

Trading individual stocks is an extremely risky method of investment, it is true that an investor can make a large amount of money in a short period of time, but the flip side of this is that they can lose it just as quickly as they made it. The stock market is extremely unstable and volatile, whether you are a beginner or a veteran investor it is not the most sensible investment option.

Stocks are traded through a stockbroker. A stockbroker is responsible for purchasing stocks on your behalf for a fee. There are two different ways that you can make money with a stockbroker:

1. Sell your stocks when they increase in value.

2. Through dividends or regular payments determined by the stock's value.

Owning a stock means that you own a part of the company; therefore, you are entitled to a share in their profit which comes in the form of dividends. Your dividends will increase when companies are performing well but when they are not your dividends will decrease.

Bonds

Bonds are similar to stocks, again you are loaning your money to a certain company. When an organization needs finances for a new project, but they don't have access to the capital that they need, they sell bonds. Investors lend money to the company; they must repay the money within a set period of time with interest. Bonds are not as risky as stocks because as long as the company is still in operation the money will be paid back at the end of the loan period. However, if the company goes bankrupt the investor will lose their money. It is rare that investors lose money like this which is why bonds can be a great investment option.

Bonds are a basic agreement to pay back at a later date. Bob and Mike could have structured their agreement in this way. It is the equivalent to saying "Can I borrow your tractor? I will bring it back to you in three hours washed with a full tank of gas" To entice Bob to lend him the food he might offer him an additional three bundles of wheat every year until he has paid back the loan. If Bob is smart he will take the offer because he will end up with more in the end.

Secondary Markets

So far we are assuming that things run smoothly for Bob and Mike and that their circumstances don't change. But since the economy is so unstable and volatile, something could go wrong. Let's say that after Bob gave Mike the loan, a swarm of wheat eating locusts came and destroyed the farm. He can't get his food back from Mike because he has already held his yearly field fallow. A solution would be for Bob to sell his contract to a third party, a farmer called "Jacob" who has a surplus of wheat. Jacob would provide Bob with corn in exchange for receiving future payments from Mike.

This type of re-selling contract is referred to as a secondary market in the finance world. Trading of this nature takes place in secondary markets such as the New York Stock Exchange. It allows an investor to sell his initial investment.

One of the disadvantages of stocks and bonds is that if you are an individual investor it takes time and money to manage a large portfolio. It was out of this problem that mutual funds arose.

Mutual funds

A mutual fund collects money from several investors to invest in a large portfolio of stocks. Every investor in the mutual fund owns stocks in the portfolio and receives a share of any investment made. Mutual funds are managed by a trained professional investor who is typically employed by an investment company.

The Value of an Investment

You will often hear financial experts talking about the value of stocks and bonds. They will generally describe them as being "undervalued" or "overvalued." The question then becomes, how are these values calculated?

Intrinsic value means that the price of an investment should be equal to its value if a buyer planned on purchasing it and keeping it without selling it. Investors who do not plan on selling their stocks and bonds are not concerned about the amount that it is trading for on the secondary market, what they are concerned about is how much they will receive in dividend payments, and from annual or semi-annual interest. Therefore, the value of a stock that has been priced accordingly should be the current value of its future dividends.

The notion that future dividends should have a present value sounds a bit strange to the novice, but analyzed through a concept referred to as the *time value of money* it starts to make sense. The simplest way to explain it is as follows: If I was given $1 today it should be worth more today than if I was to receive $1 in five years time. There are three different ways you can look at this:

1. If you were given $1 today you could invest it in a certificate deposit (CD) or in a guaranteed bank account.

2. Due to the increase in the cost of living over time, and inflation you can purchase more with a dollar today than you would be able to in five years time. For example, in the 1980's you could buy 5 loaves of

bread with $1, you would not be able to do so today with the same amount of money.

3. The majority of people have a preference for immediate gratification than delayed gratification. If you were given the choice to eat a bar of chocolate now, or in seven days, you would choose to eat it now. The point is that if you were given a dollar today, you would prefer to spend it today instead of spending it in five years time.

Due to the fact that future dividend payments are worth less in the future than they are today, a *discount rate* must be applied to express what their value is to today's rational investor.

If we have knowledge of or can observe the time value of money then we can value the price of the dollar today on the promise of $1 in five years time. What this means is that we are *"discounting it back to the present."* If we are able to place a present dollar value on the promise of a dollar in five years time, this same value can be placed on any dollar amount of future interest payments or dollar amounts.

This is exactly what is required to value stocks, bonds or any other type of investment – an estimate of the income that the investment will yield every year going forward and discount it back to the present at an applicable time value of money.

A good way to estimate today's time value for money is to look at the interest rate on safe investments such as United States Treasury bonds (IOUs from the American government). There are a range of treasury bonds; one of them is referred to as a *zero-coupon bond*. When you purchase this type of bond, you are guaranteed to receive a certain amount of profit within a specified period of time. But until that time elapses, you will not receive any interest payments. As a result of this, the price of a zero-coupon bond that will yield $1 in ten years time will be much less than a dollar today. For example, if a ten year zero-coupon bond sells today for $60 and pays $100 when it matures this means that $100 in ten years time is worth the same value of $60 today.

Why Does the Market Change So Much

Theoretically speaking, the stock market should never deviate from its intrinsic value. A volatile market can be due to three main factors.

1. **You cannot determine the intrinsic value of a company:** The intrinsic value of a company is determined by its estimated future profits and then discounting them back to present day dollars when the time value of money is uncertain. An estimate can change significantly based on changes to the economy, geopolitics, the regulatory environment, general competition, inflation and whether or not an investor is prepared to wait for a return on their investment. As a result of the dynamic world in which we live with changes to the economy taking place on a daily basis it simply isn't possible to accurately determine intrinsic value.

2. **The market is controlled by humans:** Which means that emotions such as fear and greed are all going to have an effect on the market. Human emotions play an extensively large role in what happens in the market. According to the Economist magazine, the average investor now only holds onto stock for a maximum of four months. This short holding period encourages market participants to play a game within the industry referred to by world renowned economist John Maynard Keynes as the *"beauty contest."* The objective of the game is not to try and work out which companies are the most valuable, but to work out which companies are perceived

to be the most valuable by investors. A rational investor will buy shares at a high price if they believe that another investor will purchase the shares at a higher price in the future. This can cause major changes to take place within the market regardless of what is taking place in an organization or the economy. The hope is that perception will become a reality, and sometimes it does.

3. **Reflexivity:** This is a term coined by George Soros the billionaire hedge fund speculator. The notion is that changes in the price of stocks are not only a reflection of future estimates but that they can have a direct impact on the future. An example of this phenomenon occurred recently

with the 2008 financial crisis. When the price of stocks began to decline, it was a reflection of the lower intrinsic value of assets due to the collapse of the economy. When prices start to fall, the economy deteriorates even further because businesses and households realize that the value of the stocks and bonds are going down and cut back on their spending. When large numbers of consumers reduce their spending it causes the economy to deteriorate even further which puts even more pressure on the price of investments. Reflexivity is responsible for creating extreme markets that can jump from exceptionally good to exceptionally bad within a short space of time.

The Beauty of Compound Interest

Money has got two functions; you can either save it or spend it! Spending money is more exciting than saving it and to make matters worse, Western culture encourages us to spend instead of save to in order to keep up with the Jones's. If your income is limited, it is impossible to save and spend money and unfortunately most people chose to spend it! However, the smart people who have invested in the stock market have accomplished the goal of having the luxury of being able to save and spend at the same time.

One of the most important features of getting a sizeable return on your investment is called compound interest. This means that you don't just make a profit on your initial investment. For example an investment of $100 at a 10% annual rate will yield a profit $10 in the first year and $20 in the second year. If the money is not withdrawn, in year two it will earn the $10 profit from year one will also gain 10% interest meaning that in two years your $100 investment is now worth $121. After several years of an investment accumulating compound interest something called exponential growth takes place. This means that the speed at which a dollar value grows increases over time.

At a 10% interest rate, your investment will double every 7 years with compound interest. If an individual starts saving early, the smallest investment can yield an extraordinary profit by retirement.

Chapter 2: How to Choose an Investment Account

The most important step you are ever going to make in creating an extensive investment portfolio and saving wisely is opening an investment account. You can choose from several accounts, a regular bank account, a mutual fund account, a full service brokerage account, or a discount brokerage account. When you are deciding on an account, it is essential that you analyze the associated costs. What appears to be a small annual fee can make a huge difference to compound interest. Many people opt for discount brokerages because they are made up of a combination of low fees and a wide variety of options for investment. It isn't difficult to find a discount brokerage firm because competition has caused them to lower their fees significantly.

The Importance of Expenses

I have got an interesting relationship with driving. I love the idea of being able to drive to my destination when I want to instead of getting public transportation or catching a taxi. However, I hate the stress of sitting in never ending traffic jams, people cutting you off and the threat of someone beating on your car window if you make one mistake while driving. This problem is often solved with me taking public transportation when I have a long journey to make and I justify it by the fact that it is actually cheaper to jump on the bus or train than to fill up the gas tank. The average journey costs approximately $10, however, if this price was to be increased to $1,000 I and the entire state would quickly abandon taking public transportation and my car would become my new best friend, and those who don't know how to drive will quickly learn to do so!

This same dynamic is taking place in the investment world. People are getting on that $1,000 train ride instead of learning to drive which will save you thousands in the long run. Let's look at why this is:

I am going to use two people by the names of Lucy and Paul. Both of them make an investment of $100,000 at an 8% yearly interest rate before fees. Lucy invests into a low cost index fund with a 0.2% fee. Paul invests in regular mutual fund through a regular mutual fund advisor. The mutual fund alone charges a 1.3% fee and the mutual fund advisor charges 1% to manage his investments. To Paul paying 2.3% out of his yearly assets to have someone else manage his investments professionally sounds like a really good deal, particularly when his investments are making a significant amount more than this each year. However, when the costs are broken down, Paul is losing a large amount on his returns over the life of the investment. After 30 years, Lucy would have accumulated $952,000 and Paul will have accumulated $528,000. Simply by paying 2% less in fees per year Lucy will have doubled the amount of money that Paul made. The fee that didn't seem high to Paul ended up costing him four times his first investment over 30 years. If Paul would have educated himself on mutual fund fees, he would have doubles his profits.

Let us now look at the type of accounts that are available to you:

Discount Brokerage Account

A discount brokerage account is a low cost online account offered by firms such as Fidelity, Schwab, Charles, and E*Trade. These accounts allow individual investors to purchase a wide range of mutual funds, common stocks and exchange-traded funds (ETFs). A discount brokerage doesn't have an annual fee, they make their money by charging a commission each time you buy or sell a mutual fund or a stock. The majority of brokerages charge between $5 and $15 for each trade. A discount brokerage is a low cost way for individual investors to access a range of investment options.

Mutual Fund Account

A mutual fund account is provided by companies such Vanguard, and T. Rowe Price. If you understand chain restaurants, you understand mutual funds because the concept is the same. A mutual fund account allows investors to buy funds that have been sold by their parent companies, but they do not allow investors to purchase stocks directly. Larger fund families such as Vanguard and Fidelity also provide discount brokerage accounts which means you can invest in stocks in combination with their own funds.

Mutual funds appeal to investors who want to have their investments managed by a fund manager. The down side of this is that their fees are higher, and as in the illustration we are well aware of how this can drastically cut back your returns over the long term. Mutual fund fees differ according to the company, some companies charge a fee of 1.3%, there are some that add a "load fee" that can cost as much as 5% of the sum of your initial investment. There is no good reason why anyone should pay a load fee, so run if you see it in the small print!

Full Service Brokerage Accounts

Full service brokerage accounts are offered by companies such as Goldman Sachs and Morgan Stanley. These accounts are very similar to discount brokerages except they provide a more personal service such as wealth management and advice. They are attractive to those who want to increase their knowledge in investing.

You have to be careful with this type of account because there is a high possibility that the investment advisor will recommend that you make investments that will pay him the highest commission as opposed to what is best for you. In the financial world, this is referred to as a *"kickback."* You can avoid this by having an understanding of investing for yourself, as well as looking for an advisor that is regulated as a *Registered Investment Advisor (RIA)*. RIAs have a fiduciary and legal responsibility to ensure that you make the best investments and their jobs are on the line if it is discovered that they did the opposite. Even though a broker might give themselves the title of an investment advisor, they are not under the same legal constraints.

Checking, Bank, CDs, Savings and Money Market Accounts

One of the main advantages of investing in a bank account is that there is no risk whatsoever associated with your investment. Any money that you invest is guaranteed by the bank and you can easily make a withdrawal when needed. This is a feature that economists refer to as *liquidity*. The downside is that you will not make anywhere as near the amount of money than if you were to invest in the stock market. A savings and checking account is a good place to keep money that you are going to need in a couple of years time.

Where Should I Open My Account?

Over recent years there has been a heavy boom in online brokerage accounts. Due to the competition, trading costs have been significantly reduced meaning that investors have the potential to earn more money. Large companies such as Fidelity, Scottrade, E*TRADE, and TD Ameritrade have all got good offers and are great places to start. Here are some important points to think about when choosing a provider:

- The minimum size of the account should be less than the level that you plan on investing at.
- You should be able to access online stock quotes, tools and calculators at no cost.

- No matter how much commission you generate, you should not have to pay a monthly fee for maintenance.

- You should never pay more than $15 per trade.

Once you have decided on the right provider for you the actual process of opening an account is easy. You will need all of your personal information to hand such as your social security number, and have access to the source you will use to fund your account. The normal procedure is that funds are electronically transferred from your bank account to your brokerage account. When you have opened the account there may be a few days waiting period to ensure that everything is legitimate and then you can start investing.

Chapter 3: Your Own Personal Investment Plan

If you have ever tried to get to an unfamiliar destination without a map you will know that it was extremely difficult! The same concept applies with investing, before you start making investments, you should know exactly how much you intend to make by the time you retire. From this goal, you can work out how much you need to save each year and how much you need to invest to meet this target.

Investing is Like Running a Marathon

Running a 40k marathon might sound like an impossible task to some, but millions of people are doing it every year. Often going on training programs that last for months where they gradually increase the running distance until they hit that 40k. Marathon runners have a defined goal that they are aiming to achieve.

Your expected retirement date is like the date that a marathon is going to be ran. By the time you get to retirement age, your aim is to have saved enough money that will enable you to live comfortably throughout your senior years. The main difference between a marathon and retirement is that a marathon has a finish line and retirement doesn't. It is not easy to work out how much money you will need to live throughout your retirement years but it is essential that you come up with a good estimate. The following exercise will assist you in making a decision.

The Size of Your Nest Egg

There are two major steps that you will need to take when deciding how much of a nest egg you will require to live comfortably during retirement.

1. Estimate the amount of income you will need during retirement

2. Estimate how much of your wealth you will be able to comfortably withdraw every year.

Estimate Your Retirement Income

Your first step should be to consider the lowest amount of money you could afford to live on from your investments. You can then start to think about how much money you will need in your investment account when you retire. You should think about these questions when estimating your minimum income.

- What is your spending like today?

- Do you think that your expenses will be lower when you retire? E.G. Will your mortgage have been paid off? Will you move to a smaller home? Will you have to spend less on the children? The majority of people can manage on 2/3 of their current income because there are not as many expenses during retirement.

- Do you have a retirement plan from the government or from a company? Do you think you will work part time during your retirement? Do you think you will keep working many years after retirement age? Minus any additional sources of income you think you might have when you retire. How much are your anticipated Social Security benefits? (this information is available on your last Social Security Statement).

- The number that you come up with does not have to be exact; just write it down so that you can use it for the next step.

- Do you have any goals that you would like to achieve such as buying a yacht, traveling the world or going on a cruise? Write these goals down and how much it will cost to accomplish them. Add this sum to the above total and this will be what is referred to as your *"stretch retirement income target."*

How Much Can You Comfortably Withdraw Each Year

Now that you have a rough idea of your target income, the second step is to work out how much in savings you will need to do everything throughout the year without it being a financial burden. Although you will withdraw money to meet the cost of your living expenses, you will continue to invest the funds from your nest which will keep growing. Your goal should be to have a portfolio that will last for the entire lifetime of your retirement which is typically 25 years. How much you can safely withdraw from your investments is subject to a number of things including interest rates, inflation, and future returns on your investments. Experts generally agree that:

- If you are worried that you will outlive your assets, you should make a limited amount of room to adjust your spending in case of a breakdown in the market. If you look at it from a worst case scenario, withdrawing 4% of your total investments will protect your assets.

- The majority of people should be able to make a 5% withdrawal during retirement. This is assuming that there is at least a 2% return on your investment over the retirement period.

- You may be able to make up to a 7% withdrawal rate depending on your ability to adjust your lifestyle if you experience lower than expected returns.

To work out how much money you will need throughout your retirement for your basic necessities and your stretch target, you should divide your yearly target income by your rate of withdrawal.

A Savings Plan That Will Meet Your Goals

Once a marathon runner has decided that they are going to run 40k, they have to work out how they are going to train their body in order to accomplish this goal by the date that has been set. The first step is to work out the amount of miles they will need to run each week. The rule of thumb for every marathon runner is to build up mileage each week that is twice the distance of the race, and not to increase mileage by more than 10% within a week.

The equivalent in retirement planning is in yearly savings. There is also a rule of thumb to follow when estimating how much you should put into investments each year to meet a retirement goal.

The percentage of your goal that you will need to save every year is dependent upon two factors. First the return you will get on your investment and second the amount of years that you have left until you retire.

Spread Your Investments Over Different Accounts

Once a marathon runner has decided on the date of their race and how much miles they will need to run each week to make sure that they are prepared for the race, the last step is to divide weekly miles into specific work out plans. The three main workouts in all marathon training programs are the tempo run, the long run and the speed workout.

The equivalent for a retirement plan is how to divide yearly savings into different savings accounts. Similar to the marathon training, there are three choices:

1. Taxable accounts
2. The IRA
3. 401 (k)

There is a five step process to work out how much money to allocate to each.

1. **Maximize Your Match:** If your employer matches half of your

contributions then make sure that you are maximizing the percentage of your salary that you contribute to your 401k. If the company that you work for does not match your contributions ignore this step and move to phase 2.

2. **Pay off Your Debts and Have a Three Month Reserve:** It is sensible to have cash available in case of an emergency; in this volatile economic climate you never know what can happen. You might lose your job or you might have a medical emergency. Depending on how tolerant you are risk wise you can either build your three month reserve over time or you can put all your savings in this fund until you reach your goal. If you have

credit cards or loans with an interest rate of more than 8% you should pay these off first before you start saving for your three month reserve.

3. **Maximize Your IRA Contributions:** If your IRA is eligible for tax deductions, or if you qualify for a Roth IRA, you should add any extra savings to an IRA account. If possible, get the maximum donations every year. There is nothing better than the range of choices and the tax benefits of an IRA. You should skip this step if you exceed the tax deductable income limit.

4. **Max Out Your Tax Deductibles on Your 401 (k):** The 2017 limit for tax deductable contributions is $5,500 if you

are under the age of 49 and $6500 if you are aged 50 and over. This is more than enough to build up a war chest with good tax advantages. You can skip this step if you don't have a 401 (k).

5. **Save Additional Funds in a Taxable Account:** Although this is the last step in the process, for investors with a high income, the taxable account might become the largest account because of the limitations on the amounts that can be invested in a retirement account.

Chapter 4: Asset Classes – Moving Beyond the Stock Market

An asset class is simply a group of similar types of investments. For example, if you only invested in spinach, broccoli, apples and bananas, your asset class would be "fruits" and "vegetables." There are several main asset classes, and each one of them can be broken down into industry, location, size etc:

- **Equities (stocks)** When an investor owns a piece of a company

- **Fixed Income (bonds)** When an investor loans money to a government or a company for interest.

- **Cash and cash equivalents:** The money that is in your saving account, in your wallet or under your mattress!

- **Real Estate and Commodities:** Investing in something physical such as land, property, precious metals such as gold and silver and natural resource commodities.

We can now categorize each asset class further. Just as the category of "vegetables" doesn't tell you the exact type of vegetable, so "stock" doesn't tell you the exact type of investment. Stocks can be a multinational, a start-up, American or foreign, value or growth, and the list goes on. Here are the most common ways to break down the equity asset class.

Value Versus Growth: Both of these sound great, so which one is it? Every stock regardless of the geographic location or the size of the company can be labeled as either a value or a growth stock.

- **Growth:** Think of the latest iPhone. This is a stock that is expensive in comparison to its earnings; however, investors think that the price is justified because growth potential in the future is likely to be high. A start-up with negative earnings but carry huge potential are also considered growth stocks.

- **Value:** This stock is basically on sale, the price is low in comparison to its earnings, book value or dividends. There is generally not much enthusiasm that the company's stock price will accelerate in the near future, but investors are content to hold onto it because it is a low downside risk and the dividends are high.

- **Blend:** This is a combination of both growth and value.

So now comes the task of deciding which strategy will work best for you. Opinions on this issue differ; the world renowned investor Warren Buffet is a fan of value investing, while the world renowned investor Philip Fisher is a growth investing fan. Since two of the most famous investors in the world are in support of both growth and value it is clear that they can both work. Your decision should be based on whether you are looking for a steady stream of income (value) or price appreciation (growth).

Location: Pretty self explanatory, this is where the company is based it could either be:

- In America
- Developed in a foreign but successful country
- Developed in a foreign but emerging country with an underdeveloped economy. These companies are of a more volatile nature; however; they have high returns. The BRIC countries which include Russia, China, India and Brazil are the most extensive emerging stock markets.

Market Capitalization (Large-cap, mid-cap and small-cap): Investors like to use big fancy words to describe the simplest of processes. Don't be intimidated – market capitalization is simply saying "how large is the company?" It is defined as the total value of the tradable stock for an organization (the price of the share multiplied by the number of outstanding shares). Market capitalization is broken down as follows:

- **Large-Cap:** A company that is worth more than five billion think Apple.

- **Mid-Cap:** A company who is worth between one and five billion.

- **Small-Cap:** A company with a smaller market value that is generally less than one billion.

- **Micro-Cap:** An extremely small company worth less than $300 million.

In terms of diversifying your portfolio, this is very important. Larger companies are more stable, and don't carry as much risk as smaller younger companies. On the flip side, smaller companies have the tendency for more growth potential as well as the associated risk. This is why it is beneficial to split your investments.

What Asset Classes Will be Most Beneficial For my Portfolio?

This is a very good question, and the choice is entirely up to you. There are successful investors in both growth and value stocks, large and small, as well as in physical and debt assets. Unfortunately, the majority of them are unable to outperform the market for long periods of time. As an individual investor, you can't really go wrong when trying to decide between Amazon or Apple as a large-cap growth stock pick. What is important is that you don't put all of your eggs into one basket and base your entire investment portfolio on a single asset class.

Steps to Investment Success

Asset Class Mix: The older you get, the less risk you should take because you won't have as much time to recover from a severe loss. A really effective rule of thumb to follow is to minus your age from 110 and put that percentage into bonds and the remainder into stocks. For example if you are 50 years old, 110-50 equals 60, put 60% into shares and 40% into bonds. If you want to add a bit of cash or physical assets to the mix, maybe you could slightly reduce each allocation. For example, put 50% into shares and 30% into bonds, 15% into real estate and 5% into cash.

Make sure that you don't have too much cash in your investment portfolio because overtime inflation will bring down the value of your cash assets.

Decide How Much You Want to Allocate Within Your Equities: Growth and value have had a similar performance over a long period of time. Small-cap has a higher return and a higher risk than large-cap. It is sensible to have a mixture in your portfolio. As long as you don't put the majority of your investments into micro-cap companies you should be fine.

Active or Passive Investment: Your next decision will be whether or not you want to defy the odds and attempt to beat the market or whether you want to own a portion of each stock? If you decide to go with the market index, you are a passive investor. Your choice of index fund should be a reflection of the amount of funds that you intend on allocating to your portfolio. If you made the decision to try and beat the market, you will have to put a bit more effort into it.

Independent or Professional: Many investors have their funds actively managed through mutual funds. Your money will be allocated to a range of asset classes and your asset manager will take a fee. The evidence suggests that the majority of mutual funds do not outperform the market. You can make an attempt at selecting your own stocks but you will need to make sure that you choose the right amount. You should never choose less than twenty companies across your chosen assets to ensure that you have a diversity of investments. There is no guarantee that you will outperform the market, but there is no harm in trying.

Allow Your Money to Grow: If you have made the decision to invest your money in individual stocks you are going to be tempted to sell them when their value starts to decline and to buy when the value goes up. It is imperative to your investing career that you refrain from doing this. If you have taken the time to research an investment there is no need to panic each time you see it moving. When investors buy and sell too much they underperform on the market.

Chapter 5: Real Estate Investments

There is more to buying real estate than buying a home. Over the last 50 years real estate investing has become extremely popular and has joined the ranks of common investment vehicles.

Although there is a lot of money to be made through real estate investing, it also comes with a lot of responsibility. There is much more to this type of investing than making an investment on the stock market.

Rental Properties

This type of investment is as old as land ownership; theoretically, it is a simple concept. An investor buys a property and rents it out to tenants. The investor is referred to as the landlord; it is their responsibility to pay the mortgage, maintain the property and pay the taxes. The ideal scenario is that the landlord collects enough rent to pay any associated costs. They can also charge more to ensure that they earn a profit from the property. The most effective strategy is to charge enough rent to pay for overheads and wait until the mortgage has been paid to earn a profit from the property.

The main goal is that the value of the property appreciates during the life cycle of the mortgage providing the landlord with added value. According to the United States Census Bureau, there has been a consistent increase in real estate value from 1940 until 2006, there was a dip and rebound from 2008 to 2010 and it has continued to increase ever since.

As with any investment there is always going to be disadvantages. You could find it difficult to get a tenant. You might get a tenant who for whatever reason decides to destroy the property. Any of these scenarios will result in a negative cash flow which means that you will have to pay the mortgage yourself. There is also the issue of finding a property that is suitable, you will need to make sure that you chose a suitable area with low vacancy rates and a location where people will want to rent.

The main difference between real estate investing and other investments is the time and attention that it takes to maintain it. When you purchase stocks, it sits in a brokerage account and over time increases in value. When you invest in real estate, there are several responsibilities that come with being a landlord. If the heating system stops working in the middle of the night, your tenants will call you. If you don't have any objection to being a handyman, this might not be a problem for you. The other option is to hand the property over to a leasing agency or a property manager who will manage the property on your behalf for a fee.

A Real Estate Investment Group

A real estate investment group is similar to a small mutual fund for rental properties. If you want to invest in rental properties but don't want to deal with the stress associated with being a landlord this is what you will need.

A real estate investment group will purchase or build a set of condos or apartment blocks and then sell them to investors through the company which makes them a part owner of the group. An investor can own as many of the properties as they wish, but the company takes care of the maintenance, and finding tenants for the accommodation. The company makes a profit by taking a percentage of the rent each month.

There are several different types of investment groups. The most popular is when the lease is in the name of the investor and each property pulls a percentage of the rent to protect themselves against any vacancies. This means that an investor will always get enough money to cover the rent even if the property is empty. It is up to the investor to research the history of the investment group, as with all companies there are good ones and bad ones. You will also need to ensure that you research the fees each company charges.

Trading Real Estate

This is the risky side of real estate investment. Like the day trader who is the complete opposite of the buy and hold investor, so are the real estate traders in a completely different league than the buy to rent landlords. A Real estate trader buys properties and holds them for a short period of time with the aim being to sell the property for a profit. This is also referred to as *"flipping,"* it is the process of buying properties that are weak in value and not very popular on the market.

A pure property flipper is one who doesn't renovate the house, they invest no money into making improvements, it is sold as is. It is essential that the investment has intrinsic value in order for it to make a profit without any alterations. This type of flipping is a short term cash investment.

This type of property investing is extremely risky. Pure property flippers typically don't have ready cash to pay a mortgage, if they are unable to sell the property immediately it puts them in a financial bind.

Another class of property flipper is the investor who buys properties at a reasonable price and adds value to the property by renovating it. This is generally a longer term investment depending on how much improvement is required. This type of investment can be limiting because it is time intensive and an investor can typically only take on one property at a time.

Real Estate Investment Trust (REIT)

When a corporation or a trust uses an investors capital to buy and run income properties a real estate investment trust (REIT) is created. REITs are purchased and sold in the same way as stocks and shares. A corporation has to pay out 90% of its profits through dividends to ensure that it remains a REIT. This is how a REIT avoids paying corporate income tax, whereas the average company is taxed on its profits and then has to make the decision whether or not to pay out its after tax profits as dividends.

Similar to regular dividend paying stocks, real estate investment trusts are a good investment for those who are investing in the stock market and looking for a regular income. Compared to the other types of real estate investment, REITs give investors the opportunity to invest in different types of real estate such as office buildings and malls. This means that you will not require a realtor in order to cash out your investment.

Leverage

Apart from REITs, real estate investment provides investors with a tool that is not available to stock market investors and that is leverage. When you buy stock, you are required to pay the full value of the stock as soon as you place your order. Even if you are making your purchase on margin, you can't borrow as much as a real estate investor.

The majority of conventional mortgages require a 25% deposit. There are a variety of mortgages that are dependent upon your location; some require as little as a 5% down payment. This means that you have control over the entire property as well as the equity that is in the property by paying only a fraction of the total value.

Landlords and flippers can take out a second mortgage on the property and then pay a deposit on other properties. Regardless of whether the properties are sold immediately for a profit or they rent them out, the investor is in control of these assets even though they have only paid a small percentage of the total value.

The Benefits of Real Estate Investing

There is no such thing as an easy road to wealth, there are going to be obstacles and hindrances regardless of how you choose to make your money. However, it's not all doom and gloom, real estate investing will provide a substantial amount of wealth in the long term. Here are some reasons why you should invest in real estate.

Cash Flow: After the mortgage and fees have been paid, there is typically some money left over for you to play with. It will provide you with a passive income that you can use to either reinvest, travel, or build another business.

If you have a reliable tenant, cash flow as a real estate investor is much more predictable than the majority of other businesses. This is great news for entrepreneurs enduring the hardships of a start up. The cash flow can get you through the bad times and enable you to live well during the good times.

Tax Benefits: If you earn $500,000 through your own business, and I earn $500,000 through investing in real estate as a rental property owner, who gets to keep most of their money? I do! As a rental property owner you are not required to pay self employment tax and the government provides tax benefits including:

- Depreciation
- Lower tax rates for profits in the long term

Increase Your Net Worth: When you purchase a rental property, your tenants rent is paying your mortgage which increases your net worth every month. Due to the loan paydown, a rental property is basically a savings account that is continuously growing without you making a deposit.

Today you might owe $300,000 towards a rental property, but next year you may only owe $295,000 because the tenant is making your payments meaning that you are $5,000 richer. Twenty five years down the line, your mortgage is paid, you own the property outright and you can either continue to rent or sell it for a profit.

Appreciation: When the economic climate is favorable while the loan is being paid off, the value of the real estate is going up. This is why it is essential that if you decide to get into real estate you do so for the long term, as this is the only way to make a good profit.

Protection Against Inflation: Can you imagine paying five dollars for a bar of candy? Or ten dollars for a loaf of bread? While these prices seem ridiculous, this is the nature of inflation and we can't escape from it. While the majority of people fear inflation, rental property owners look forward to it.

When the price of a loaf of bread hits ten dollars, the price of everything else also increases and this includes rent and property values. The one price that will stay the same is fixed rate mortgage payments. As inflation causes the cost of living to increase, cash flow for the landlord also increases.

Control: If the rental market starts to get more competitive, you can start advertising more, if value goes down, you can renovate a part of the property to justify an increase in value, if you want to find a better deal, you can go and look for one that is more suitable to your budget!

The bottom line is that you can control your own financial future by investing in real estate.

How to Begin

Depending on what country you live in, there are rules and standards that you will have to follow before you can start investing in real estate. Since I am writing for a majority American audience, that is where my focus will be.

Anyone can become a successful real estate investor if that is what they want to do. It takes a combination of getting educated, finding a good broker to help you to get established, and determination. Here are some important points to get you started.

Get Educated

Regardless of the state that you live in, you are required to take a pre-licensing course. Each state has their own requirements so you will need to check with the licensing board to find out. For example, the state of California requires you to take three college level courses. Idaho requires you to take 90 hours of classes split into two courses. Some real estate agencies have additional educational requirements, so you might have to take some extra courses before you are hired by an agency.

Choosing a Brokerage

A real estate brokerage is the office or agency which brokers and real estate agents work. Since it is required that you work with a real estate broker before you can branch out as a real estate agent, you will need to start looking for a suitable broker prior to graduating from your training course. Brokers have a minimum of three years supplementary real estate training, they will be able to assist you with any questions you may have concerning working as an agent.

When looking for a broker, consider the size of the brokerage, the reputation that it carries and the extra training that it offers. You can check the reputation of the brokerage by reading reviews online and asking others directly who have used their services.

You can also get more understanding about brokerage through your interview questions. Spend time carefully constructing your questions to get the information that you need to determine whether or not you would want to work with the agency. Here are some questions you might want to consider:

- Is there an additional coursework requirement?

- What is your level of experience? How many years do you have in the industry?

- Will I have an assigned mentor that I am constantly working with?

- How do you develop leads? How do you make contact with your clients?

- What is the average amount of time it takes to start earning a commission?

Getting Your License

You will need to pass state and national exams to get a real estate license. You will also have to provide a criminal records check. Though prices may vary according to the state that you live in, you should expect to pay a minimum of $200 to get your real estate license.

A Real Estate Agent Budget

If you want to become the best at your craft you are going to have to make some investments. You should expect to pay between $1,500 to $2,000 which will cover your licensing courses, signs and advertising, business cards and association fees.

To start off as a real estate investor, you will be paid on a commission basis only; therefore, you will need to set money aside to ensure you are able to survive just in case you don't start making commission straight away.

Join an Association

You will need to join the National Association of Realtors (NAR) in order to use the title "realtor." You can do this through selecting an affiliated brokerage and attending a certain number of meetings established by your local chapter.

Develop Your Client/Referral Portfolio

The most effective method of building your client portfolio is to use your own personal network and to get a mentor. A mentor will guide you through the real estate profession establishing contracts and splitting the commission. You can also ask friends and family members to connect you to people that they know who are planning on buying or selling their home. Someone is always looking to buy a new home, and that one referral could be what kick-starts your career as a real estate investor.

The Bottom Line

As a real estate investor you will need to learn how to find the best deals, how to analyze the real estate market, and how to find a sustainable method of financing your investments. Essentially, it is a business and you have to treat it as such. As it grows and matures you must ensure that you nurture it. You are not going to start making passive income immediately, but as millions of real estate investors have discovered over time, there are incredible rewards to those who are patient.

Chapter 6: Investment Tips For Beginners

As you have learnt through this book, if you want to build wealth, saving a percentage of your monthly earnings is never going to be enough. One of the most important decisions you will ever make is to start investing. You can apply the strategies throughout this book to start building the financial future that you deserve. Before you begin your journey, here is a reminder of some essential tips:

Prepare Yourself to Start Investing

Before you put a cent into an investment market, you will need to ensure that you have got everything in order. The pioneer of The Mathematical Investor website Mark Morelli advises that you start by setting a monthly budget, this should include all irregular expenses such as taxes and insurance and 20 percent of your gross earnings should go towards savings. Your next step should be to pay off any loans and credit card debts. Your final step is to build an account for emergency funds.

Ask a Professional to Help You Set up Your Account

Setting up an investment account if you are new to investing can be overwhelming. Julie Rains publisher of Investing to Thrive recommends that you get the process started by calling the customer service department of a brokerage firm. There are trained representatives who will answer any questions that you might have. They are not qualified to give you investment advice, but they can point you in the right direction that will assist you in making your decision.

Begin With Simple Investing

Certified public accountant Mike Piper and the publisher of ObliviousInvestor.com is famous for his simple but intelligent approach to investing. He states that keeping things simple is the most effective way to invest. Whether you are investing through a retirement plan at work, an IRA or both, your contributions should be automated each month. You should also find an all in one fund that has a low maintenance fee and an allocation that matches your risk tolerance. This way you are killing two birds with one stone saving you some time and minimizing the amount of mistakes you could make.

Set it and Forget it

Certified financial planner, certified public accountant and fee only wealth manager George Papadopoulos advices that first time investors who typically only have a 401k plan at work should choose a target date fund, set their investment goal and leave it alone.

Dollar Cost Averaging Investment

Dollar cost averaging involves transferring a specified amount of money on a regular basis into an investment account for the purchase of stocks and bonds. This is a disciplined approach that pushes you to purchase more shares when prices are low and fewer shares when prices are high. You can practice this strategy by investing in a 403b or a 401k.

Don't Invest Large Amounts of Money

You don't need to have a large amount of money to start investing. However, it is advised that you begin with small amounts to get you started. Rains states that you should purchase a mutual fund with no transaction or load fee, set up purchases automatically or invest randomly whenever you have extra money. Companies such as Schwab have index mutual funds with initial minimum investments of $100.

Keep Your Expenses Low and Diversify Your Portfolio

Certified financial planner and pioneer of Future Perfect Planning Cristina Guglielmetti suggests that first time investors should keep their expenses to a minimum. Even if you have a great year with high returns a high expense ratio can cut into your profits, therefore keep your expenses low by choosing an index fund that is broadly diverse, make a comparison of yearly fees and choose the cheapest. The amount you pay in fees is important because it can make a huge difference to your returns over time.

Companies such as Fidelity Spartan, Standard & Poor and Schwab provide access to low fee index funds.

Ignore What You Hear on TV

You don't need to follow the financial market news and listen to the advice of financial commentators to become a successful investor. CNBC is not your personal investment advisor. Guglielmetti states that new investors should refrain from heeding the advice of TV financial spokesmen because they only provide short term advice and if you are going to be a successful investor you will need to be in it for the long haul.

Get Investment Ideas From Social Data

If you have knowledge on public opinion about a popular product or a certain company you can use that information to assist you in investment decisions. Casey suggests using social data as a platform to collect ideas for conventional stock research methods. For example, over the past couple of years, there have been multiple unlawful shootings by police officers, when terrible events like this happen; people start to talk about it on social media. One of the suggestions was that the police should be forced to wear cameras. If this idea is implemented by the police authorities, stocks in the company who supplies the cameras would immediately go up providing a good investment opportunity.

Invest in Stocks Free of Charge

There are several ways that you can invest in stocks free of charge and the Robinhood app is one of them. The app doesn't charge anything to trade stocks. However, the only disadvantage is that it is riskier to invest in individual stocks than to invest in a diversified portfolio of low cost index funds.

Realign Your Investment Portfolio Yearly

When you start your investment journey, it is advised that you select an asset allocation reflecting your risk capacity and risk tolerance.

After you have set your preferred asset allocation, ensure that your portfolio is rebalanced every year to make sure that your original allocation is paid back.

Don't Put a Timer on the Stock Market

Owner of Peer Finance 101 John Hogue gives the following investment advice. This especially applies if you are new to investing because it will only confuse you and cause you to abort your goals early. Don't waste time trying to follow technical charts and timing the stock market. Since you are an amateur you should play the game like one, that isn't meant to be an insult it's simply the truth of the matter. Don't try and bleed out every returns percentage from stocks by analyzing and trading. Finally, he says you should choose investments in companies that have products that you love and will be around for the foreseeable future.

Would you ever take your hard earned money and throw it in the trash? I am sure the majority of you answered NO! Making an unwise investment is the equivalent of throwing your hard earned money in the trash. It is imperative that you do enough research before parting with your money. Don't just choose different investments for the sake of being diverse do your research first. He also advises not to waste money on short term investments since the stock market is too volatile. You should make sure all your investments are for the long term with a minimum of five to seven years.

Make a S&P 500 Investment

According to the founder of Money Under 30 David Weliver, every beginner should make their first investment in an index fund that tracks the Standard & Poor's 500 index. There are several funds that you can choose from through a broker; his favorite choices are the following:

- iShares

- SPDR

- Vanguard

The S&P 500 market index keeps track of 500 of the most prominent stocks traded on the Nasdaq stock exchange and the New York Stock Exchange. These stocks are stable, large and are representative of a cross section of the American economy. Weliver claims that by making an S&P 500 investment instead of the whole stock market you minimize the volatility and risk that comes from the stocks of companies that are smaller and not as established.

Weliver advises that a first time investor should focus on making long term investments of a minimum of 10 years. You shouldn't buy stocks that you are not comfortable with holding if the stock market were to crash for five or 10 years.

Over a long period of time S&P 500 index funds should deliver large returns greater to or at least equal to those of the most actively managed mutual funds. They also do not carry as much risk as individual stocks. Combined with the low expense ratios, these funds make the most viable investments for beginners.

Conclusion

I am hoping that you have come to the end of this book with the following:

- An understanding that investing is not as difficult as it has been portrayed.

- Most importantly, the confidence that you will be able to apply the principles that have been outlined in this book and build a solid financial future for yourself.

It is important to understand that building wealth does not mean accumulating a lot of material possessions.

Wealth is stability it is having the confidence that your family will never experience lack because there are resources available to get them out of any physical constraints they might find themselves in. It means that you can send your child to the best schools and give them the best education so that they can continue to build wealth. Wealth means that you can sleep comfortably at night knowing that you are in need of nothing, your family is in need of nothing and that if an emergency should arise you have the ability to attend to it.

It requires dedication to build wealth, even if you were born with a silver spoon in your mouth or you have come into a large inheritance, your parents or your grandparents had to work exceptionally hard to get what they have today.

There is more to wealth than just having money in the bank, it is a particular way of thinking, and a discipline that the majority of people fail to master in life which is why only 2 percent of the world's population hold the majority of the worlds wealth, they chose to be different and follow the road that leads to wealth and not poverty.

Wealth is also a relative term, I am certain that Bill Gates would be horrified to have $1,000,000 in the bank, but to the average Joe that is wealth. Regardless of your perception of wealth, you chose to read this book because you are either tired of living from hand to mouth, or you are concerned about the financial legacy that you are going to leave for your children.

Education is a perquisite to wealth, it requires a solid understanding of economic principles, constant self evaluation, lifelong learning and training. Reading this book is the first step to educating yourself on the basics of investing. As long as you use the knowledge that you are reading, you will succeed in your pursuit of financial independence.

Other books available by K.C. Smith on Kindle, paperback and audio:

Taking Destiny Steps: Learn How to Live Your Dreams

Everyone Screws Up: Learning To Forgive Your Stupid Mistakes and Recover With Grace and Humility

The Essence of Power: Learn How to Tap into Your Personal Power

How to Handle Cowards, Thieves, Liars and Manipulators Without Breaking The Law